Maryland Bards Poetry Review

2020

Maryland Bards

Maryland Bards Poetry Review

Copyright © 2020 by Maryland Bards

www.localgemspoetrypress.com

Edited by Nick Hale & James P. Wagner (Ishwa)

Table of Contents

Fran Abrams

Highly Developed Humans

In the year 2135, people no longer
will have vocal cords, no longer
will speak. Highly developed
humans will communicate only
with devices attached to their wrists.

If you want to call your children inside
for dinner (thank goodness, children still play
outdoors), you need to message them
it's time to come in. Message again
to wash hands and face before
coming to the dinner table (thank goodness,
families eat dinner together). At the table,

there is no chatter of children's voices.
In some households, the use of devices
at the table is strictly prohibited. In others,
families send messages to one another
while they chew and catch up
with the events of the day.

Highly developed humans learn
to read at the same age they learn to walk.

1

Before that, tiny devices attached
to their wrists make soothing
cooing sounds to let them know
their parents care about them.

The ability to hear persists.
Highly developed humans want
to listen to wind in trees, rain
on window panes. And music.

Highly developed humans do not hear
voices raised in anger,
snide intonation of sarcasm,
tender tones of love. Symbols
in their messaging software
substitute for spoken emotions.
(Thank goodness, humans still have
emotions.)

Fran Abrams, Rockville, MD, began writing poetry in 2017. She has had several poems published online and in print. She was a juried poet at Houston Poetry Fest in October 2019 and a featured reader at DiVerse Gaithersburg (MD) Poetry Reading Series in December 2019.
    Visit franabramspoetry.com for more about her work.

George Angell

2131

I saw our blue-eyed ballplayer's apotheosis
from bleacher section 96 in right. Five bucks
to watch Game Two One Three One (W-Mussina,
16-8; L-Boscie, 6-4) that night
when schools in Baltimore had just reopened
and summertime was digging in its heels. Euphoria
was levitating neighborhoods and marble stoops.
Inside the ballpark, pandemonium was trapped
and caged, but wouldn't stay contained. Not
    past frame four,
when Boscie's fastball, mashed against the ash
    wood barrel,
sprang off and sent a violent, mortar pulse's shockwave
of jubilance. Cal trotted Cal-like. All the rest
was only after-party. Stooped, the emissary
of games in yellowed clippings, Joe DiMaggio,
pronounced the benediction of the superseded
who loped in pinstripes through Elysium's grass.
    The four
great canvass digits dropped, confetti black and orange
rained down through pig fat smoke from Eutaw.
    Clutching babies,

fans at the railings strained to touch the hem of Jr
when he had slipped the concrete dugout's mortal bonds.
Ramrod and weathered, Sr stepped unbothered past
his old eviction's site, the coach's box, more giddy
than all the limo-litter VIPs, more giddy
than all the big league regulars who grinned the grin
of kids in t-ball caps at the colossus Cal,
more giddy than the umps who didn't make the slightest
attempt to dam their adulation up—men who
had punched the air derisively year in, year out
to teach their zone du jour to straight-backed
    Number Eight.
Above the Yards the moon turned on its Big Top beam
and, all the while, the tribute that was easily
the best kept flashing from the board beneath the porch
aloofly through the scenes of downright storybook
and choked-up words: …*OAK 1 BOS 3 …
    CLE 4 *MIL 1 …

Originally from North Carolina, Mr Angell has lived in Baltimore since 1982. He is married and has one son. His undergraduate degree is from Princeton University; he subsequently earned an M.A. in Classics from UNC-Chapel Hill. In spring 2019, he retired after a career of 37 years as a translator, analyst, and reporter with the Department of Defense.

Melanye Ann

Event Horizon

To touch my soul
You must first steal my heart
The path to my heart is through your eyes
An event horizon
In an unlikely disguise

Melanye Ann was born and raised in Baltimore and is a hairdresser and Reiki healer. As a self-taught artist, she expresses herself through multiple media.

Allison Arinaga

I Live in a Place Between Two Worlds

I live in a place between two worlds
That rarely fit together.
And though it's fun
To mix and match,
It's hard to be a tether.

Every time I stretch one side
I'm forced to turn around.
Without a world
To call your own
Identity is drowned.

But in that middle void, I've found,
Is where new culture's grown.
So take that space
Between two worlds
And claim it as your own.

Allison Arinaga grew up in Montgomery County, Maryland and is currently pursuing her Ph.D. in chemistry at Northwestern University. She also enjoys many non-science hobbies such as reading fantasy novels, studying foreign languages, and writing poetry.

Frank Asher

Alone~Aloneness~Lonely

Alone time~Lone Wolf.

You've got to do this alone..You'll never walk alone.

Grief can be lonely~alone with grief.

The lonely hearts club.

The Lone Ranger....

Alone again, naturally.

When we engage do we acknowledge each other in order to balance the lone scale?

We are born alone(sort of)

We die alone. (Sometimes)

And..It's a journey one can only take alone.

We are hardwired for social engagement!

That's what helps us survive~sometimes it helps us live longer lives.

"Wherever you go, I will follow you".

It's lonely at the top..It's just as lonely in the gutter.

We are not ALONE..

Well, where are you?

WIll I be going this alone?

My journey had to be taken alone.

Yet, so many held space and heart for me.

This alone thing can SUCK...Mostly because it is a

figment of my own making.

Making it alone doesn't really make it better~simpler maybe~but not better!

Being with myself doesn't have to be alone by myself.

BY MY SELF...I stand with my SELF..

That's a full, lovely and loving place to start.

Zaimat Bayero

Failed Love

But tell me,
How heartless can you be?
I tell you I can't live without you; you tell me I'll do
just fine
I say my whole world revolve around you
I tell you how much it will hurt if you leave
But you tell me it will hurt just for a little while
You say I am strong so I can overpower it.
How heartless do that sound?

I only enjoyed eating because I get to share food with you
Enjoyed walking because I get to hold hands with you
I only enjoyed sleeping because I get to dream of you
Enjoyed talking because the subject is always about you
I only wanted marriage if I was married to you
Gave love a chance because I wanted to experience it
with you
So how heartless can you be not to realize that I am
only living, because I am currently living for you?

So, tell me,
How cruel can you be?
Just for you to ignore all the memories you made with me
Why would you make plans with me if you are just going
to cancel it?
Why make empty promises that you know you can't
fulfill?
Why would you watch me fall as hard as I did just for you
not to catch me?
Why would you say words to me if they meant nothing
to you?
Why would you look me in the eyes when your eyes
lack sincerity?
Why would you let me have a taste when you are not
interested in sharing a future with me?
How cruel is it that you made me give a part of me to you,
that you plan not to return?

I now have tears in my eyes all because of you,
Stopped eating because it doesn't taste good without you
Stopped walking because my hands feel too heavy
I stopped sleeping because now my dreams are nightmares
Stopped talking because there is nothing more to
talk about
Marriage seem overrated all of a sudden
And love? That just hurt so much
Now simply living, remind me of you and since you
are gone

I don't enjoy it quite as much.

But tell me,
How much of a monster are you?
How much pain could I have caused you?
How much hatred could have been in your heart?
How long have you been holding It in?
For you to let me fall this hard
And you refuse to stop me from falling
But you didn't catch me either...

Zaimat Bayero, is an 18 years old college student majoring in Biology and minoring in creative writing. Zaimat is an aspiring pediatrician and poet. Zaimat started writing at the age of twelve as a way to speak when she has no words and escape from her thoughts. Zaimat hopes to publish many books and poetries in the future aiming to giving hope to everybody needing a little more encouragement!

Alisa Berger

2 AM

Evading me
slipping around the tree trunks
Peeking between the long blades of grass
romping through the meadows

settling on me like a feverish child
suddenly straying distracted by some obscure fun
laughing and teasing sliding from my pillows

My eyes flash open
wide awake
full of worried truths
pebbles
rattling in my brain

Unhurriedly, unexpectedly,
tiptoeing in
wrapping me in her warmth
till,
again,
capricious sleep
slips away

13

Alisa Berger is a poet and teacher. She is inspired by the joy, pain and the magic that is found by listening deeply to the memories that surround us. Her hobbies include walking, drinking coffee and painting with friends.

Maggie D. Brace

The Darker Side of Faeries

Faeries cavort about the pond,
'neath the shade of frilly frond.
Bedecked in dewy crown of jewel,
they attend their Faerie school.

Learning their magic must be hard,
with knowledge of both plants and yard.
They must be gentle, kind, and firm,
managing bird, bug, and worm.

Affixing lacy flower to stem,
each fragrant bloom, set as gem
atop the verdant, spiky spire,
plants that grasp ever higher.

Curling tendrils upon grape vines,
nestling cones amidst the pines.
Inviting dragonflies to tea,
briskly dancing 'fore Queen Bee.

They must study plant, corm, and root,
teach young owlets how to hoot,
weave a dewy chamomile rug,
polish bulb of lightning bug.

But not all tasks are equal met.
Gruesome chores we oft forget:
Nipping bits off butterfly wing,
coaching horny toads to sing,

drilling the pill bug how to curl,
coaxing stinkweed to unfurl,
creating slime for sluggy trail,
guiding skink to shed its tail,

imbue dung beetle's love of poop,
turn dead carcass into goop,
It seems like magic, oh so fun...
Faeries' work is never done!

Maggie D. Brace is a lifelong denizen of Maryland, teacher, gardener, basketball player and author. She attended St. Mary's College of Maryland and Loyola University, Maryland. She has written 'Tis Himself: The Tale of Finn MacCool and Grammy's Glasses, and has both tied with Anne Tyler in the Baltimore Sun Paper Reader's Choice for best local writer as well as lost out to John Waters. As heady as this sounds, she remains a humble scrivener and avid reader presently aging gracefully in situ.

Michael Wayne Bright Jr.

(Queer Grace)

A way of a kind
Yes because of no
Grace is free
Giving in to the impossible
An immeasurable somehow
Rather than die
Hearts
Tender in nature
Tence to the touch
Too heavy to just take away
To full to just put away
Make a double jump
Rebounding higher heights
Rebelling in love
Because life won't wait
All by the grace
That is new this day

Michael Wayne Bright Jr is a native of Anne Arundel County. He is an aspiring theologian and poet. He is a 2015 graduate of Lancaster Bible College, and a 2020 graduate of Lancaster Theological Seminary.

Alice Brooks

Laughter

You have to laugh at yourself.
Life is funny. You don't get
what you expect. And you
don't expect what you get.
You don't have what you
want. And you want what
you don't have. You don't
need what you got. And
you got what you don't
need. You don't laugh
when it's funny. And do
laugh when it's not funny.
Isn't that funny???
Isn't that life???

Alice Brooks has been a resident of Maryland since she was a baby. She is retired and enjoys reading, writing, being involved with various forms of arts and crafts and beginners pickleball. Her greatest joy is watching her grandchildren grow up, being positive and studying the Bible.

John Busby

the dead rest Gently...Softly...expanding out into the Universe...

Creating Life

the Happy Children Playing in the Garden...
Sun Shining down upon all...

there's a Song playing somewhere far away...or is that just
in Your mind...

some of the gravestones are crooked...the Mary Mother
statue is new and shiny...there's a Red Rose at Her feet
that Someone must have put there...it's made out of
plastic...maybe it'll last forever...

fear of what could happen keeps You a prisoner from
acting on Your True Feelings...

the fear of Your entire World falling away...

there's a Red Cardinal just looking at the Sky as He stands
on a crooked gravestone...
He wonders at the sounds...it's White Cloudy...but the Sun

is out also...cold and somewhat warm at the same
time...cars going by here and there...People going some
where...

no Leaves on the Trees...
I wonder...sitting with the dead and the Living...
the everlong silver thread that connects to all...

I Give Mother Mary a wave goodbye as I get up off
the bench
say goodbye to the plastic Rose
wave to the gravestones and tell Them all that I Love
Them

then I turn and head down the road

Onwards my Friends
Onwards...

Will Carpenter

What Happens by the River

The dealers appear on the pavement by the pier
from midnight to three—disperse with the cops
and come back when the cops leave. The high
schoolers fuck in their trucks and Toyota Camrys
from four to five. Old Al owns ten to sunset
with his rope of writhing catfish, doesn't bother
hoisting them up until he's done fishing perch.
Newt and his wife Nancy drop by from time to time
in Grateful Dead T-shirts with a homegrown joint
    between them
and slow dance to the waves lapping tar-slagged pilings.

We all have our time. Mine's roughly sunset,
when the river turns artery, the reeds over in Prince
    George's County
dye strawberry blond. This is Steve's time, too,
now that he's out on bail and black mud smells
like freedom. We come with burnt, bare feet, warped
fishing rods, dirt-cheap cigars and cheaper beer,
plus extra to swap for bait and conversation. We
    sling lines
left and right for fear of snagging the sunken VW Bug in

front of the pier
(some say motorcycle, some say bus, but Bug is the
    consensus)
and if we catch a blue cat we'll fry it; Fish and Game
won't bother us because they're listed invasive.
We come at the overlapping: Al and Newt, high tide and
    water snakes
and children screaming from inner tubes.
We come for the grand portrait. But once

I came before sunrise to taste the bated breath
of pre-dawn, the still gray before a runny sunrise cracked
above the tree line.
I stripped down and slipped silently under the quiet
current, which drowned a father two months before,
leaving my truck unlocked and my clothes draped
    like flags
on a fishing-rod-holder.
But I came up.
I came up gasping and echoing
through a quiet world, startling a blue heron.

William recently graduated from Penn State with degrees in Philosophy and Political Science, and is currently pursuing an MFA in poetry at the University of Florida. Though he has relocated throughout his life, he calls Calvert County, MD home, and much of his work explores the question of what it means to be from a given environment.

Ananya Chand

Lines and Curves

Distorting
Contorting
Deforming Within the walls of my throat
My stomach churns
With its contents planning an escape
My lashes, my soldiers, intertwined with one another,
Try to block the passage to the outside
But fail
So much as if it'd have been the same
If they weren't there at all
The air blows and a narrow strip down my cheek
My lips
To my neck Is cold
My tongue tastes the salt
And my entire mouth becomes sour

All of a sudden
It all becomes too much
For my soldiers to handle
And they become drenched

As the storm worsens

And the rain falls fast and hard
Feeling like little bullets
And children struggle To cover their soft skin
I flood my mind
With the words
Of the last song I listened to,
Masking my thoughts,
Muffling my screams,
So I don't have to think them

And everything stops

Everything is still

Being a step near normalcy,
My fingers pick up the blue pen again
Blue lines and curves on the white
Minutes pass and my fingers let go to reach for my eyes
My soldiers are back at work
And my throat becomes lines and curves

As a young adult, born and raised in Maryland, about to embark on the terrifying yet exciting journey of college, Ananya finds herself facing a lot of emotions internally. Poetry is her way of understanding and expressing them. When she's not writing, she practices the culinary arts, as she plans on majoring in food and beverage entrepreneurship. Her lifelong dream is to own a restaurant inspired by the multicultural environment she grew up in, wanting to share her Indian heritage with others.

Greg Clarke

Brats on the Beach

Rising before dawn,
requires stamina and brawn.
Gear-laden vehicles filled to the rims,
a stop for fresh coffee, covered to the brim.
A short trek to the Assateague dunes, always a site,
hoping the sea will provide a tug and a bite.
Portage of equipment across morning sands is quite a feat,
strength is preferred but good for the weak.
The pounding of the morning surf, bringing the tide to rise,
each wave that laps the shore leaves a momentary surprise.
Lines are prepared casted into the depths,
stationary sentinels of monofilament resting between reps.
Sunrise and sea spray combine,
to repeat a fishing tale older than time.
A morning meal is prepared above the sand with gas
and grill,
The aroma is familiar, each sense it does reach,
A meal fit for kings...
Brats on the Beach!

Greg Clarke was born and raised on the upper Chesapeake Bay and holds a great respect for those who came before. Many of his travels and experiences can be seen in his ability to write and represent nature as the true spirit it is. He has been recognised for his contributions recently in the Sand Dune Poetry Anthology, 2019. Similar writing can be viewed on his blog, observeinspire.home.blog or on google at : The Hunter's Muse, Nature Writings.

Ellen Coffey

Bathtub Madonna Blues

Bathtub Madonna
in a digital world.
Lopsided, out of place,
mired on a muddy spot
in a weed chocked front yard
where grass no longer grows.

Houses, once shining
and swollen with
fresh paint pride,
like a worm fattened robin
preening on dew soaked lawn.
Now ramshackle, spent,
old leather scuffed shoe,
worn at the heel broken.
History's misfortunes
moved in to stay,
heedless of past glories
and bygone fame.

Forgotten on a stately edge,
faded town with city dreams
hope rocks you in tender arms
calling you her pretty child,
though you have not been
that for many years.

And yet,
like a bathtub Madonna
you are still here.

Ellen Coffey is a poet and retired Marketing Manager living in Cumberland, MD. She is president of the Cumberland Chapter of the Maryland Writers Association and a member of the Cumberland Poetry Roundtable. Her poems have been published in Pen In Hand Magazine and in Poets Choice.

Signe' Coleman

In Rain

In rain, she cries
To hide the blood of broken dreams
The thunder muffles her screams
There is no sound
No one around to see
Her hopes flee
The storm rages on, cutting her compassion
Every kindness is her last one
Prayers for the ending ring in her ears
No one to hear
There's fear, of herself
What is there, in her heart, beyond shadow?
How long can she light their fires with her candle?
They share no light, no warmth
Admonish her for sitting in the dark
She's grown used to it
Fused with it
Forever one, the shadows are at peace
But she has no rest, she cannot sleep
There is no release, no ease of tension, of pain
She cries, in rain

In vain
Standing in ashes of dreams long since slain
Hands shaking with cold as she tries to meld them together
again
She cannot
It's not meant to be
She's not meant to see
What's bright, what's beautiful, what's light
What's happy, what's right, what's life
Her door only opens outwards, never in
No one ventures within
There's more to her
If she could find it
In time, if she could rewind it
Break apart a family
Before she could be
Before that first cry of tragedy
All she holds that no one can take
Is that last breath
From her lips, it must come
No one else's
With this, she has no choice but to be selfish
A broken heart, struggling lungs
But her screaming isn't done
In rain, she cries
To avoid telling lies
To avert her eyes
To confuse the spies

She plots her demise
In her imagination
What is the sensation
What is the time
Another day, far away, for her sake, for their sake
She stays awake, awake, awake, awake
For her sake, for their sake
She cries, in rain
And shadow
So they won't know
So they won't go
So it won't show
So they won't know
So they won't go
So it won't show

Signe' Coleman is 28 years old and lives in Salisbury, MD. She enjoys writing poetry based on personal experiences and sharing them with others. She has been writing stories, songs, and poems ever since she first learned to write.

Mike Collins

See This

Junkie wailing-mart shoppers pushing carts of
China white goods, the heat of first/last/only dollars
spilling from their veins to be left lifeless and dead by
bank pushers helicoptering to Hampton stashholes,

Neutered men staring through beerandashot eyes
at padlocked gates of factories long idled by suits with
smooth hands and smoother lies of investment and profit,

See This

Screen glazed children's eyes searching for
meaning in an ever flowing ever growing web
promising/delivering ever more data but ever less truth,

Never forgiven debt choked students educated to
ignorance
their numbers charted for profit, gasping/grasping papers
declared irrelevant by corporations,

See This

The gaping mouth of a world strung out
on burning furnaces sucking through
an ever narrowing oily black straw,

the filth of tar sands exposed to the very sunlight
that makes it unneeded/unwanted
by any but those who would profit,

See This

Brothers in stairways sisters in parks
runners with hands held high all murdered all lost
in cities outlined/defined by that thin blue line
drawn with hatred and guns,

The knee of oppression pressed casually
in to the neck of any man woman or child
deemed not sufficiently compliant
not sufficiently white,

See This

Families hopes kissed one last time and sent
North by parents seeking only to save them
from poverty hunger and the grasp of narco fueled thugs

greeted here by spittle spewing forgetters
of their own families arrivals,

Brown skinned dreamers seeking only to join others
long here and long ignored
their backs forever bent in the fields of plenty
and in the gardens of those who hate them,

See This

Doublespeak masquerading as law
Whores masquerading as politicians
Corporations masquerading as people
Warlust masquerading as patriotism
Greed masquerading as charity
Sex masquerading as love

We see all this
and yet still we continue
to let small minds divide us
to put dollars before people
to put hatred and malice before love.

Michael is a resident of Cecil County and has written primarily for the theater for over fifteen years. His plays have been produced at several local community theaters and he has written and produced the show, *Ghost Walk in Chesapeake City,* for a dozen years.He also writes and produces segments for Cecil.tv, a local web based Television Company.

Mel Cort

Intermeddelers

I don't know if everyone
Is pretending that they're not there
Or if they
Don't see them at all.
But they stay,
And they won't let me forget this,
Hovering,
Watching,
Their colorful judgment cocooning in the empty space
in my brain.
I wanted to fill it with something
Worthwhile, love or
New knowledge or
Something other than them,
But they sit nestled and I carry
Them with me.
Just me, my backpack, and the things in my brain.
Sometimes they try to get out.
Desperate to be seen, heard, felt by another who wasn't as
used to their flapping
As I was.

As I am.
They don't pay rent,
My little mind roommates.
I'd complain, but they won't let me.
So they stay,
And I carry them with me.
One day,
They whisper on nights
When they don't let me sleep,
One day,
You'll break. We'll break you open,
And we'll be free.
Everyone will love us so!
They shout, pressing at the edges of my skull and
fracturing the seams.
Everyone will love us,
and forget you,
Broken on the ground.
One day.
But for now,
They finish,
Carry us.

Mel Cort is a full-time high school student at Mercersburg Academy, where she studies poetry at every opportunity. She is a three-time silver key winner for the *Scholastic Art and Writing Awards* with work featured in *The Online Journal of Exceptional High School Writing*, *Blue Review,* and local publications. She is a Maryland native.

Kevin Coyle

Tree

Trees stand still
Laboring silently within
Their branches

Reaching to the light
Some leaves remain
Attached, changing in color

Others fall free
They cascade down
Decomposing

Leaving their nutrient gift
Nourishing life once more
Chemicals released

Break the silence beneath
Aiding the survival
Of the other

Growing sometimes fast
And sometimes slow
They have rings to show

Their sum combined
That outlast us
Bearing a record of the past

In silence they stand
Offering Nature her beauty
And each season, a new page

Kevin Coyle is a freelance writer from the Frederick, Maryland area. Apart from writing, he enjoys photographing Nature where he finds inspiration for his poetry. He hopes to someday put his poems to music.

Thomas DeCaro

Death Haiku

Grey black stir clouds
Boil away East.
Snow! From a clear sky-

Natasha Donoway

The Coin

Half White
Half Black
So where am I at?
I get on the bus
prepared to sit
Struggling to find out
where I fit.
You can't sit over here
You're not one of us
but you can't sit over here
you're not dark enough.
Whom shall I date?
Whom shall I marry?
Which injustice do I carry?
which side of the war
Do I see myself on?
which side of my heritage
must be dead and gone?
Which half of myself
Should hate the other?
Am I mad at my father?

Or mad at my mother?
these questions I have
don't relate to just me,
these things are tearing apart
OUR COUNTRY.
Half White
Half Black
So where ARE WE AT??

Natasha Donoway is a 40 year old poet and activist from Sharptown, MD. Natasha has been writing poetry since she was 15 as a way to express herself and her feelings. She discovered as she got older that she could use her words to bring awareness to various social issues plaguing our country in an attempt to reach people that she may not have been able to in her everyday life. Poetry is her medium of expression, there are no rules, only emotion. Natasha lives her life in between the lines on the pages of her journals and continues to seek the words to enlighten.

Richard Epstein

Iambic Monometer

    I've lived
This life
    Took wife
Knew strife
Stood tall
Leaves fall
Paid rent
Back bent
Lost son
Work done
Can't talk
Can't walk
It's time.
I'm done.

Richard Epstein is a resident of Silver Spring, MD. His poetry is his attempt to examine and understand our environment and our place within it.

Kristin Ferragut

Like It's New

The lonesome in being young sharpens.
Coming of age in the 80s, the older
look at lips of those younger like murder.
Parents won't share a sip, even if it's alcohol.

One hundred thousand dead and dying.
An epidemic feels just like a pandemic if
you're in the wrong place at the wrong time.
Two am at Boothill Saloon Cemetery can't be

the right place except when I knew
he shot crack through his veins and I might stop him.
I suppose we all want to die a bit anyway, especially
me when he eluded being found. Invisible like viruses.

Still we hunt in sideways looks at others, supposing
the cleanliness of fingernails or shape of eyes might
expose harbored sickness. Harbor grudges

for the skateboard thrashers, always at the parks sharing
hi-fives and Pepsis. Selfish youth in congregation
of laughter and risk, intent on killing us all. As though

it's not the time of their lives.

Neat with pockets to hold cell phones not fistfiuls
of quarters, husbands, second husbands, cats, dogs, debt,
music and the ceaseless bad news. We hide in our homes
and act as though we've never seen a plague before.

Kristin Kowalski Ferragut writes, teaches, plays guitar, hikes, supports her children in becoming who they are meant to be, and enjoys the vibrant writing community in the DMV. Her work has appeared in Beltway Quarterly, Nightingale and Sparrow, Bourgeon, Mojave He[Art] Review, Anti-Heroin Chic, and Fledgling Rag among others.

Suzanne Ferrone

Loving You

Loving you excites me, ignites me, delights me,
And makes me want to fight you...
Im living in your shadow
Waiting for the afterglow
That I fear will never come

You astound me and confound me,
Turn me inside out and ground me.
When you need me all you gotta do is call...
Oh my Lord, you're my downfall.

I love the way you touch my soul
The way I lose my self-control,
You are the whiskey in my glass
And I fear that I wont pass

This test of self-restraint
You intoxicate, and stimulate me
Aggravate and intimidate me
The decisions I make and the actions I take
Will lead me back to you

Abigail Freeman

Midnight

A lover under dark of night
A maiden in the day
Her love saved for a withered soul
Who loved from far away

A blue as black as moonlit night
She stumbled from the east
West, he lay on scattered star
but always out of reach

She sang
Love me till the break of dawn
Love me till your all but gone
Love me like the rising sun
Love me more than anyone

In frigid crisps the wolves replied
With rotten skin and swollen eye
They howled, growled, drooled to feast
And said don't fear the starving beast

She screamed a screech, satanic sign
He heard her plea her battlecry
He ran away, from end of day though panic he confessed
I'll never love you from afar should I escape the west

And as he found the sacred sound
but of what he wanted least
He sank in sore to woodlands core
Light glare off sharpened teeth

he sang
Love me till the break of dusk
Let me be the one you trust
Love me let me hold you so
Love me till i let you go

Abigail Freeman is a writer from Maryland currently attending college at Maryland Institute College of Art with an interest in animation and film. She enjoys writing poetry in her free time exploring magical and surreal themes to tell her story's.

Kate Gaston

West Rogers Avenue

The landlady says they usually bloom in May,
But here it is June and the air sits heavy with their
particular scent.
Yesterday I walked outside to pick one of the blooms
off the tree.
The front walk was still rain-puddled and slick from
the summer storm
Which had rolled up and over the Chesapeake Bay.
 The thunder is still a low rumbling growl in the back of its
throat as it passes on further north.
Reaching way up high, standing on tiptoe to grasp the
lowest bloom, I broke its stem;
The suspended raindrops showered down from the dark,
waxy leaves.
It looked glorious in my brown thrift store vase.
But those blooms sure don't keep.
Waking this morning, I found it had thrown wide its petals
in unconditional surrender,
The seeds spilling down freely, wantonly, cupped where
they fell in the soft white flesh of the petal.
I lift the bloom, careful against the mess of seeds pouring
out

But they do anyway, fairy-dusting the tabletop with their fine, golden pollen.

Intending to toss it out into the overgrown side-yard, I pause by the back door,

Lightly fingering the odd texture of that petal.

And just like that I'm back;

A tomboy climbing a magnolia tree under the hot Alabama sun.

Embraced within that shadowy green half-light,

I shimmied outward on the branch to gain the prize, a blossom full-blown.

Plucking it, and clambering down one-handed, I brought it to you.

Inside the house was cool and dark, the windows thrown wide open to the breeze.

You smiled and gave the bloom a jarful of water.

You gave it pride of place in the middle of that old kitchen table,

A heavy wooden thing, shrouded ignobly in its perpetual spill-proof vinyl cloth.

It is in the heart of a child always to bring flowers,

Offerings on the altar of affection.

Receiving your quiet benediction over that fast-wilting bloom,

The peace bestowed on that child remains full as powerful to the woman;

As tangible now as the petal, silken and surrendered between my fingers.

Kate Landry Gaston is a recent arrival in Baltimore, Maryland. Originally hailing from Alabama, with stops in Utah and Connecticut along the way, she has immediately felt a kinship with the candid warmth of Marylanders. She is trained as a physician assistant, and worked in the University of Alabama at Birmingham's trauma and burn center for eight years prior to ping-ponging across the nation for her husband's residency and fellowship. She currently home-educates her 8-year-old daughter, Addie, and enjoys the quiet rituals of daily life in this new city.

Lennon Gross

Conium Maculatem

Come Spring and we'll find you
In Ophelia's bed
Pearls wrapped 'round
Your slender neck

Or laid bare in the garden
'Neath full April moons
Ensnared in a memory
Of philosopher's kiss

Neglecting at times
That call - like a lover's
To relish in anguish
A torchlight
A sin

All of my life
I've been looking 'round corners
Your face and the darkness
Are all I can see

Lennon spends their time writing, drawing and traipsing the wooded hills of the agricultural reserve. They are a designer by trade and graduated from Frostburg State University in 2018.

Pam Haas

Or the Hunger

I feel skinny

like the night you dumped me
when we were meant to be
consummating my birthday dinner.
I lost my appetite and went home
sick the next day from some kind of ache

There weren't cravings that looked the same
as the outline you left me behind
—but still I shrunk and felt more the bump of bones
covered with skin and concave with empty

and still I crave for anything to fill me
the way you had before we went to bed
at night and again in the morning;
(when something was missing)
I couldn't tell if the pain in me was you
gone

or the hunger.

Pam Haas is a Towson-based graduate student and full-time service associate currently rediscovering her passion for tea and poetry. When there's no pandemic, you can normally find her working on her laptop in a local cafe or walking her roommate's dog at the park.

Zachary Hanks

The Return

Am I trying or simply dieing once again
It feels as though this time I won't be returning my friend
Suffering from the same crime of disbelief of my own
afraid i've ventured far into the unknown
now lost drowning in pain and sorrow
in the darkness with no light to follow
Lost in the void I cannot find my light
It seems so far gone in this dimly lit night
If I was ever in the father's graces
surely now their seems no traces
For in my race to find what I surely tried
I abandoned fate and left myself to die
A fool am I to not have seen the signs
Telling me that I've been repeating time
The circularity the Deja Vu
I fear I could have stopped if I had tried too
Could have avoided this world of darkness by knowing the
worth of my own
But alas I struggle still in the depths of the unknown
Now it seems my chances have run thin leaving nothing but
doom

Nothing but apologies left in the room
I'm sorry to myself for letting you down
I'm sorry to God I can see your frown
I'm sorry to all of the people I may have hurt
Only hoping I won't be sorry by time I disperse
Is this the real world or is it the other
regardless my suffering is not at the hands of another
But only a part of me sitting here all alone
The cold I've created is surrounding drowning me sinking me
like a stone
For what you create you will receive
Though in fact it was myself I did deceive
There is a way to return from these sorrows
To return this pain to the depths from which borrowed
I only hope I find this fate
and pray for my life that I am not too late
I have tried perhaps not quite enough
As I truly do feel that I be not enough
How could I expect to do it all alone
When all are here to find their former home
Though I have seen many faces
I fear I am not looking in the right places
So I ask Truth to hear my cries
To once again allow me see the sunrise
The Sun again and the Love of friends
Please God turn my soul right side up again

Zachary Hanks was born in Gaithersburg Maryland moving to Cary North Carolina as a toddler he then moved back to Columbia, Maryland in 2000. Zachary continues to live in Maryland to this day. He has always enjoyed writing though has not pursued it until more recently. He love animals and enjoys making glass artwork

Ashlyn Hinzman

Mystic Pearl

I kissed the top of your head and told you goodnight
I didn't know I should've been telling you goodbye

Your body was cold in the morning
Ten years later, I'm still in mourning

I carried your picture with me everywhere I went
Gracie kept searching for you, still smelling your scent

She sat by the window, waiting for you to come home
Thanks to her, I was never alone

I always called you my angel, now you really were
No one could've prepared me for how much this would hurt

You came into my life at the start
Now your name's tattooed across my heart

You were reunited with Logan, he was mom's best buddy
We used to play out in the woods and get all muddy

You've welcomed many others to the Rainbow Bridge where you wait
One day you'll welcome me through the gate

Poe, Lilly, Amy, Nick, and the ones you never met

Last year
I held Luke as he took his last breath
When Gracie took hers, I sobbed into her neck

Their deaths were planned, I had time to prepare
I gave them each chocolate on the way there

There's a picture of the three of you that made me weep
I know you all watch over me while I sleep

Talking about you still makes my voice break
Losing you caused more pain than I could take

It was the straw that broke me, and I started to slip away
But the others comforted me every single day

I think you'd like Chloe, she's so sweet and kind
Puff is full of life and has your eyes

Tonks is my problem child
But she and my boys can always make me smile

Lucy still goes on adventures
Jasper still tries to chase her

Axel has given me scars
Hope has the purest heart

Ramsay came out of the blue
Lola and Lacey came as a pair of two

I wish I could go back, redo that night
I'd hold you in my arms, not let you out of sight

Ashlyn is 24 years old and has been writing since she was 10. She was born, raised, and still lives here in MD. She has written close to 150 poems and her main topics are mental health, trauma, recovery, empowerment, love, and heartbreak.

Lynn Holmes

ECT – It Works

Oh, it's not what you think.
I know what they say.
The legends and stories
could scare you away.

No straps involved,
No restraints employed.
Not even a mouthguard.
No manna from heaven,
No endorsement from Freud.

A cute little mask to deliver the twilight.
Off to dreamland go I.
Fraction of a minute, they tell me.
Relaxed, reposed, tranquil, no cry.

Not sure if it's working,
takes time to reveal.
Has my depression lifted?
My new world, surreal.

Three times a week.
Four weeks and done.
Turning the corner.
Unload the gun.

For 20 years, Holmes inspired middle school students to explore and discover themselves through poetry. Now, in retirement, she attempts to do the same for herself.

Alison Jordan

Writing 2018

Thoughts trickle down the pencil,
Soon the trickle is a stream
A steady stream upon the page,
Who knows where it wanders.
Perhaps a deer will drink,
Of the stream flowing by;
Dragonfly larvae hunt within.
Tiny pebbles made ever smaller,
By the flow and lazy tumble;
Of ideas old and new.

Alison Jordan lives in Gaithersburg, Maryland with her family and seven adorable chickens. She is an active member of the local Irish dance group Ring of Kerry Irish Dancers. Alison is also a Quince Orchard Library volunteer and a retail worker in addition to being a poet.

edward klein

dreaming of skipjacks

I was dreaming of skip jacks
I was dreaming of the bay
I dreamt I was a waterman in the waterman's heyday
thanks to captain bart murphy my dreams come to pass
I dredged oysters on his skipjack
nearly froze off my ass

It seemed so romantic in the books that I'd read
but words can't describe ten degrees
with the wind blowing twenty
and the deck freezing up
it was hard being a waterman one day was enough

We went out on a push day
the weather it was rough
then he put up the mainsail
it smoothed her right up
she looked so majestic
I had to pinch myself to feel
if I was dreamin
or was it all real

We dredged by the bay bridge
And didn't do a thing
then he put her on some oysters
and slowly they came in
six hours later we docked with just 22
a little more than pocket change
for a five-man crew

Then he told me of the days they'd be in by one
with a hundred fifty bushels those were the days they had
some fun
but the oysters are dying now and just can't be found
said he may be leaving tilghman
find work in the town

An era is ending the skipjacks soon will be gone
but the captains and their stories will always linger on
when I'm singing of the bay
no set is complete
if I don't sing of the skip jacks of the
chesapeake fleet

It seemed so romantic in the books that I'd read
but words can't describe ten degrees
with the wind blowing twenty
and the deck freezing up
it was hard being a waterman one day was enough

ed klein, born and raised in new york city, now a resident of st michaels, has been writing about the chesapeake bay watermen for the past 30 years and is still fascinated with their way of life

Christine Kouwenhoven

The Colors of Mourning

The colors of the cards on the center hall table are blue
the blue not of a clear cloudless sky
but as it is in Van Gogh's paintings of apple blossoms
the blue of tears perhaps, or dreams

The colors are lilac and pale green
Every color is soft and the things that are drawn
on the cards, the flowers and birds, are airy and light
hinted at with gentle brushstrokes only

The colors are pink and the lightest yellow
Tender words are written on fragile translucent papers
that might easily dissolve, as if the sadness could too
if just whispered about in watercolor

I am so grateful for all of this kind comfort
this idea that grief is a gentle thing that might in time
fade to a palette of heavenly pastels

but outside the blue of the autumn sky is steely
and the leaves on the trees – orange, red, yellow –
are bright sparks that might set the world on fire

with a missing that will be difficult to extinguish
The wind that is whipping them about has an edge
and the sharp sun seems almost desperate
to offer its last light before a crashing darkness

These are the colors this morning
These are the colors of this mourning

Christine Kouwenhoven lives in Baltimore, Maryland where she works as the Grants Manager at the Enoch Pratt Free Library. She's a poet and essayist and has had pieces appear in a variety publications. She has an M.A. from The Writing Seminars at Johns Hopkins University.

Hiram Larew

Undone

If I unteach my kiss or unwake my morning
And star the days that rise beyond
If I reach back to where the newness lives
And firsts flowed by
If I undo my done-ings
And near the point of dreaming
Get there and then come back to now
With any gathered loops or straw long gone
If I but ever.

If I return to us
And unteach my kiss or untime my shirt
Or unhum arrows
If I begin again all over
If I act like onions do in Autumn
And love surprise as if it plunked the surface
If I unteach my lips to dwell
And if all that or more becomes my taken for granted
If I unteach my kiss
If I unlearn my every now of you
To swim.

This poem first appeared in Poets and Artists.

Larew's poems have appeared widely and have been nominated for several Pushcart prizes. His *Poetry X Hunger* initiative is bringing poets and poetry to the anti-hunger cause (PoetryXHunger.com). He lives in Churchton. On Facebook at Hiram Larew, Poet.

Monica Leak

She Breathed

She was the beginning
Forming the heavens and the earth with nurturing hands
Rocking it like a baby with lullaby calling it from void
to form
 As night covered the deep places of the baby's dimples
and her movement swept over the waters
She was the beginning

Then she inhaled and exhaled and breath became word
Word became light
Light separated from darkness
Word became water
Waters separated from waters
Word became earth and seas
Vegetation: seeds and trees
Word became ruling lights of the day and night
Living creatures on land and sea called to multiply

She was the beginning
She was Word, Word with God and Was God
In the beginning with God

She breathed
Acknowledging the good of her creation
Speaking blessing of fruitfulness and multiplication
Evening and morning become days
She breathed and it was good

She inhaled and released breath and word together
Making decision for creation of humankind
In her image and likeness to rule and have dominion over
the creatures of the air , sea and land
Yes humankind she shaped from the clay of the earth in
her own hands
And with her breath, humankind became a living soul

She was the beginning, all things exist because of her
Without her would nothing have come into being
In her was earth, fire, water, wind ….life
Her life was the light of all
Her light shone from the darkness in the beginning
Never did the darkness overcome her light

Because she breathed I am
Capacity that will not be crushed
Destiny that will not be denied
Poised in my priesthood

Being perfected in my purpose
Prophetic voice beyond value
To speak life and breath into my sisters
Inhale, exhale, RISE and breathe.

Monica Leak is a school-based speech language pathologist in Charles County and a seminary librarian. She was 2018 DC Poetry Project Finalist and a 2019 judge for the DC Poetry Project. Her first collection of poetry, *No More Hashtags Remembrance and Reflections was published* in 2018 and its follow up *No More Hashtags: Who You Calling?* in 2019.

Jane Leibowitz

Sea Play

If you were a sea creature
And I were the ocean
I would surround you
With warm currents.

I would be your refuge.
I would be your home.

Sometimes I would sweep you
up in my wave,
Twirl you, whirl you,
Hold you, roll you,
Then rush you to shore,
Leaving you beached and dazed.

Jane Leibowitz lives in a town near the ocean surrounded by trees, birds, critters and her husband – everything she loves. Having been a graphic designer for 20 years she found it difficult to refrain from illustrating her poems but...words first! She is a foodie, who lives to cook, a photographer and is finding lots of time now to hone her drawing and painting skills.

Angelo Letizia

Drunken Philosophy

Condemned in my drunken sleep
The starry gavel
Echoes through the universe
I must stand at attention
And face every star
Every planet
And volcano
The ice caps and dust particles
Rivers and soils and trees
All of the pieces of the universe
That somehow turn red
And flow into me
Channeled out though my wounds
The involuntary artery of heaven
Standing on trial, at attention
Now on the operating table
A broken bed
A bar

I must endure the treatment
And as I get dressed to go to dinner
I realize that
The universe is simply
A germ

Angelo Letizia moved to Maryland in 2018. He currently resides in the beautiful hills of Manchester Maryland in Carroll County. He is a college professor by day and poet by night.

Darren Longley

good enough

deep dark September night
a friend's living room floor
  and I watch you sleeping
I see your chest rise and fall
I feel your breath on my skin
  and how to tell you
  how to let you know
I'm scared of the man
who wants to love you
who wants to lose himself in you
    never feeling good enough

that deep dark September night
so afraid of loving losing you
  oh, how to hold onto you
I see the truth behind your smiles
I sense the doubt in your kisses
  but how to tell you
  how to let you know

I'm scared of the woman
who won't let me love her
who refuses to lose herself in me
   never feeling good enough

Jack Lynch

Stikes Holler

It must've been a crooked little old man
with a bundle of sticks tied to his back
who built those leaning plank buildings
and simple country houses perched on the hill
stuck in a mountain crevice
above creek and rails
that's Stikes Hollow

two cricks run down alongside the mélange of barns
granary and shed structures
rushing spouts of whitewater
dropping dazzlingly down the slope

although I had gone by it a dozen times for years before
I hardly, really noticed it, now it catches the eye every
time I speed by along the curves of creek and rail
I was too busy watching the Virginia Creeper roll
towards West Jefferson, clicking and clacking along
blossoming black clouds, flowery smoke of burned coal
maybe the engineer at the window would wave back

it all still stands like determination

that hard little gap born from a verdant vagina
stubbornness in a startling wood slant
defying gravity and laws of physics
daring the wind to blow hard
hiding the inner mountaineer strength
and the endurance of a thousand storms
and hard times and simple homespun joys

we are Appalachia, we stand here bent to your eye
our world needs no straight, or firm, or flush
prop us up on rock, the heights, the spring waters
sustain us
bring on another hundred generations
unless our judgment call comes from Christ
we'll be waiting here
planting or rocking or picking, weeding, sewing a patch
almost timeless as groundhogs
hiding in these mountain holes
and blinking in the sunlight
as you whip by us blaring your horn

Jack Lynch uses poetry to reflect upon his Appalachian heritage. He grew up in Alexandria, Va., went to college in Greensboro, NC and did a year in a MFA program at George Mason University before settling down in Baltimore for twelve years, and has recently lived in the Frederick, Md. area for twenty years. He is married with two children.

John MacDonald

Made of Glass

We, old friends and lovers,
pay the tab, leaving Eric,
estranged and drunk, at the bar,
to walk you to the car.

He says he'll see you later.
We pretend that's true.

He loves you too much.
That is his downfall.

You love him too little.
That is your downfall.

And so this last luncheon dissolves like
the surprising, fleeting, late March snow
that greets us at the restaurant door.

Outside, we pretend
not to say goodbye to you.

You are thin. You are pale.

Your clothes hang loose,
too heavy for you,
but they keep you warm,
and disguise you.

You don't seem worried about him.

You'll get a ride to your parents'.

"It's better there. I'm not lonely," you say.

We are always alone, I think,

but today we are walking down the sidewalk together.
Today we are walking down the sidewalk and I can see
your footsteps are made of glass,
not flesh or beak or bone but glass.

They settle on the sidewalk
like melting ice,
beautiful like you,
in your lavender knit cap,
and ambulatory IV drip,
that slips
from out your sleeve,

and I can see your footsteps are glass,
not stone or shell but glass,

and you say, "I may break,"
which is what we all should say
but now you must because
it's true.

Your fingers are translucent fragile and I can see the
bones, light passing through them.

You were blown hot red hot, set in a kiln until you cooled.
The steps you take are glass,
not clay or mud or stone but glass.

All of us are glass, pretending we can't be broken but you
said,
"Yes, I may break."

You said it. "I may break."

You said it. "I may break."

"I may break.
I may break.
I may break..."

And now I'm sure someone
walking just behind us sees
the glass footsteps
we both make.

John MacDonald is a lifelong Marylander, born in Salisbury, raised in Rising Sun, and now living in Silver Spring. His poems' themes often explore the environment and people of Maryland, and he strives for honesty over portrayals of beauty. He has been published in numerous magazines and journals from the Chesapeake Bay region, including Gargoyle Magazine, The Doctor T.J. Eckleburg Review, and Poetry Journal.

Kim Malinowski

Amethyst Tornado

The tornado amethyst is a slice
of stalactite formed at the roof of a cave—
drip-by-mineral drip
each drop forms another ring.
The slice is polished on both sides
and each crystal, each ring is visible.

> He takes it from me,
> holds it in his palm,
> his face reflects in stone
> shadowed, eyes dark.

Tornado amethysts mean hidden inner growth;
secret expansion of the higher self.

> He says, "pretty"
> > the same way
> > > he says "pretty"
> > > > when I twirl in ruffles and lace.

If someone took a crosscut of me—would they see each

drop of calcite?
The opaque center,
the crystalline quartz middle,
the split center where the drips all stopped
and sand and madness seeped in.
Would you see the green of disappointment?
And the deep purple that would make me
amethyst?
Each drip of magick and manic, captured,
glittering in stone.

I take back the amethyst cupping it close to my heart.
"Pretty," is okay, but I want to be majestic,
transformative.
I want my tornado self
to be weighty in your palm
and have you embrace each drip.

Kim Malinowski earned her B.A. from West Virginia University and her M.F.A. from American University. She studies with The Writers Studio. Her debut poetry collection "Home," is forthcoming from Kelsay Books. Her chapbook Death: A Love Story was published by Flutter Press. Her work has been featured in Faerie Magazine and Eternal Haunted Summer. Her work has appeared in War, Literature, and the Arts, Mookychick, Black Poppy Review, Calliope, and others.

Donald L. Marbury

Mama On God

Duquesne Power and Light
Foreclosed on our 60-watt sun
And we found ourselves bathing
Not so much in the ebony air, but
The gloom that momentarily
Slipped from Mamas eyes
As they blinked
Through an empty change purse

And she lit a candle,
Placing it on the mantle,
And we cowered from the shadows,
From the flickers of movement
That infiltrated everything
That had minutes before been familiar

And I knew she was going to pray
And I didn't want her to
We were mad: no light, six kids, Daddy's sick
And if she don't hit tonight...no money
She was going to pray

95

And I didn't want her to
Better to talk to Duquesne right now
Than God

Yet she began, and I tried not to listen,
But heard anyway, and soon it seemed
She wasn't praying at all, but
Giving a lesson
So leaning over the candle
She began to slowly pronounce

"If I exhales too hard,
If my movements is wild
Or the least bit forgetful,
If I don't guard against
The outside forces then
My light would be extinquished and
I would be put again in darkness
Blind, powerless, trapped and alone

If its life-giving things is took away
If cause of some sassy desire
I meaning to or accidentally knock it over,
If I position myself wrong and block its lumination
Then my light would be useless and I would be
Dulled and lifeless, confused and alone

And as this light outside
So be the light inside
Which must be
Nurtured and protected, shared and seen.
My light of the world
Is yours children
Ya can attempt to hide it

Smother it or deny its being

But unlike this flame here
It'll re-ignite
And reshine with sparkling embers
And a blinding hot wick
Allowing all who need and
Desire its path-guide a reprieve

"Light outside,"
Mama gently stroked the flame
"Light inside."
And she suddenly squatted and
Let us look directly into her eyes
"The same kinds of forces
Is working constantly
On both

But if the water, neglect, exposure or
wind do cut off your light."
She blew out the candle.

"Aint it nice we know of a constant flame
We can use to relight our own?"
And she slowly relighted it from a matchbook

Then we cried,
Because we couldn't watch television and
The candle shadows
would not go away

But mama hit
And Daddy got well
Duquesne got paid
And we shut our fuss
And a candle today
Seems a lot cleaner,
Much brighter,

More protective, and
A great deal more loving than
A sixty watt bulb.

Rev. Marbury is a long-time, Maryland performing-artist poet and a former national public broadcasting executive. He is also a former professor of film and television at Howard University and an adjunct professor of English, reading and writing at Montgomery College. He left the vice presidency of programming at the Corporation for Public Broadcasting in the mid-1990s to answer a call to Christian ministry, and has been an AME Church pastor for the last 25 years.

Allan May

Loss

Sometimes the memories come like snow,
and then melt, transformed
to the same water that makes up my body,
present but not noticed.
How else can I go through the days? And tell me:
will we really meet again? And how many times
did we meet before, lifetimes ago, that I cannot remember?
Is hope merely vanity, an ambition I feel obliged
to pursue?

The sun rises and sets every day, the tides ebb and flow,
and I still look at the stars absolutely amazed, though not,
perhaps, as much as I used to. I understand how rare
this planet is, how inevitable that it will end one day;
yet I hesitate to take even the smallest life, to destroy
what I know is only the briefest flash in an infinite night.
I cannot not care, cannot give up all happiness.
The hole you left is an emptiness, but the emptiness
is an invitation as well as a farewell.

I choose to see you everywhere, to feel your soul
like breath, like the wind, like light. I choose

to live happily, to not drag you into grief,
which has become a soil where new life still will grow,
and to rise each day like the sun, which loves the world
unconditionally, shining on everything and enduring
beyond the darkest cloud.
And like the dawn, the knowledge rises in me:
I honor you more with joy than with grief, more
with hope than despair,
more with belief than with doubt.
I will survive this loss
and we will meet again.

An English major and editor of the Univ. Texas at El Paso literary magazine *El Burro* in 1967, C. Allan May, Jr. has been writing poetry for over 50 years. Born in Texas and growing up in New Mexico, he has lived all over the United States, working in medical and technical writing, information technology, and management consulting in both private industry and government. He has a master's degree in Public Administration, is an avid photographer, and enjoys finding beauty in the world, both in his photos and in his written work. Allan has lived in Maryland for the last 24 years.

Jamal McCray

I Made Love to the Sun

Glorious rays of the sun enlighten the day;
I chase you through the trees,
I chase you through bramble and brush;
Beautiful fluctuations of reds, yellows, greens, and oranges.
The sun has come down into my abode,
She is most resplendent to my soul.
I feel her depths, her warming glow.
How long shall I chase what I cannot catch?
One minute you are nigh,
The next you are over there!
Peeking out at me, from in between the leaves.
How can I catch you?
How can I attain such a beautiful one?
Perhaps she is not meant to be caught,
   One cannot possess another,
So I must simply abide from afar;
My thoughts in languish tearing me asunder,
In joy, in happiness, in marvelous wonder.
One day I shall know the sun and we shall create beautiful
Planets together.

Jamal McCray is 28 years young residing in Brandywine, Maryland. He graduated from Bowie State University and has self-published six books. He currently works in D.C in the hospitality industry and enjoys the wonders of nature.

Daniel Meoli

I'm trying to get like you

I'm trying to get like you
 I wish I was a kid again
Passed out in the back seat of the car and waking up to you
carrying me to my bed

I'm trying to get like you
And tell people what to do and how to do it
And I wish I never did some of the things I chose to do
But I'm getting better everyday
Even tho it's not something you say very often
I know you're proud in a way

I wish I was a kid again
So I could be less of a brat
 to the man who's hard work paid for my clothes and put
food on our table
I'm sorry.

I wish I was at your job
hustling your co-workers in the break room
Playing pool
Skipping school

trying my best not to act like a fool

But then again you probably would've never gotten
that raise
If you spent more time at home
And I'd get a lot more done
If I spent less time in my head

Daniel Meoli is a 26 year old musician, artist, and writer from Elkridge, Maryland. He is a student at Howard Community College and plans to finish his bachelor's degree at a University in Maryland. Daniel finds inspiration from his dreams, photography, and various struggles in life. Daniel is constantly looking for ways to help the world through creative outlets. His goal for his work is to inspire others and simply to express himself. Daniel is grateful for the opportunity to share his work with others.

Stacey Merola

1000k

Fireflies twinkle
Grace a gift amongst the angst
Christmas from insects

Stacey Merola, Ph.D. is an educational researcher and program evaluator living in Chevy Chase, MD. When not working she enjoys taking her son on adventures, running, playing piano, and contemplating fireflies.

Mikayla Mislak

I Don't Want to Be Predator, and You Are Not
My Prey

It feels wrong to be a woman
and like women.
It's like the sloping edges of my hip bones
can be sharpened into a cage.
Like the lioness in my blood is hungry
and I'm hunting for perfume splattered onto the
same curves
that break my back and make me look down at my shoes.
I am not born with violence
but violence found me when he took my neck beneath his
palms
and tried to figure out how hard he could squeeze.
I am not ready to pursue my fellow doe. I don't want
to break off some young buck's antlers and use them
as my own.
Those contests of dominance were not made for me
but my arms are only big enough to hold her
and not strong enough to protect her.
I would gladly throw my whole body to their dissection
if it meant that she wouldn't be exposed to the blades
of their leers.

But I still crave her.
My hands
aren't big, and my body
is soft
but I can still cut through her clothes with my eyes and see
the sinew that surrounds her heart.
When did sex become a dirty word?
When did we start pinning it to a wall
and splitting it open to see its insides?
When did we start to violate it with gory slang like
"Screw her"
"Ram her"
"Bang her"
"Pound her"
"Nail her"
Sex is a war I want no part of
and yet I still want to touch her skin as badly as I want to
hear her history.
I would never force her
manipulate her
contort her into a shape that can fit beneath me
because I know what it feels like
to have your bones stretched like putty and your
legs ripped apart
so that they can reach inside for that precious part of you
and carve it out until you're so hollow
that you don't know how to scream.
This desire to be intimate

to share our bodies as a way of kissing each other's souls
has been tainted like roofies in our drinks.
If she ran from my desire
I would understand because I have been running for
so long
that my lungs are filled with acid and my legs
are on the brink of collapse. I know
that unwanted attraction can be just as terrifying as hate
So I will never ask anything of her.
I will never ask anything of her.
I will
never
ask
anything
from her.
Because I'm a woman
and I'm in love with one too.

Mikayla Mislak is an assistant acquisitions editor at Rowman
and Littlefield Publishing Group. She lives and writes in
Baltimore City.

Victoria Mullins

2000's

I remember a mother's day
Back when I was young
Picking flowers in the backyard
To place inside a mug.

Most of the flowers were
weeds but
You couldn't tell.
By her smile, it was

A bouquet of roses
The best assortment yet
Because they were picked
With love, a thousand pieces met

Her dazzled eyes and mouth
Split wide, teeth showing
At the breakfast tray in front of her:

A coffee, toast burnt black,
and flowers in a mug.

Victoria is a very direct poet. She writes from her heart and includes her personal experiences to give her poetry organic depth and meaning. It is natural, raw, and full of feeling.

Justin Osborne

Shadows and Fog

Sun across the sky.
Shadows following opposite ground
Torn away, look around.

Clouds move in, painful sound
Shadows, skys, hidden ground.

Thunders rage, lighting bolts
Fists clenched and chains taught.

Sheets, blankets of furious rain,
Downpours, wash over pain.

Settled, quiet. Dripping drops.
Fog is risen, moving stops.

Watch for shadows, listen for sound.
Lost in fog, search around.

I won't give up, until you're found.
I know you're out there.--

Justin Osborne is a lifetime Maryland native. Father of two. His poetry reflects unspoken elements in the contemporary, family dynamic. In his attempt to raise awareness to Parental Alienation.

Carlo Parcelli

More Funhouse East

Like something out of an Austen novel,
    An introduction by Dr. Rudd Fleming
To one John Pauker, Esquire,

And this son of an immigrant barber
    Was off to the More Funhouse East
On Porter Street, Washington DC, circa 1970.

At Yale, Pauker with the reactionary poet
    Reed Whittemore and the
CIA spook-to-be James Jesus Angleton

Published the lit mag, Furioso, which included
    The fashionable fascist poet Ezra Pound
And his sentimental alter-ego William Carlos Williams.

Soon, the barber's son was sipping martinis
    And holding court with men in tailored suits
With promises of publication and travel

Who seemed more of the fifties of his childhood
    Than the 1960s right outside the door.
Catching on what was expected of him,

Voice of America, Eastern Europe, Cold War.
    But he declined their overtures,
Refused their publications and reading tours.

Jump 47 years to a dive bar in Middletown, CT.
    The Corner Pocket Bar and Grill.
The Beat Poets, our poet's latest refuge,

That as his wife says, "Get him. His vulgar energy."
    That smack of old country pig farmer
That can't be bred out.

It's hot and crowded, and a bunch of the regulars
    Mid-libation have been trapped by a poetry reading.
And as the poets read, the barflies grouse.

Then the barber's son, dressed in a robe and abaya
    Startles the audience back to the First Century,
The time of times of that most infinite asshole Jesus

Who like the folks at the More Funhouse East
    Knew nothing of living's worth, proposing nonsense
That only made living a hell on earth.

Dramatic, biting, standup, Lenny Bruce funny, a dervish
    Wheeling about the bar, pounding on the pool table.
Wild eyed, grabbing startled patrons by the collar.

And spitting literal spit the words of Oranius –
   "A golden age a peace and love?
Seen any a that about?!!"

Or Barabbas – "As Pilato confirms, no more secure
his throat
      From me dagger,
Less the barber, takin' strength from me,
         Strike the blow.
      So may the Antipas go the way of Janneus, and
The Hellenes and Herodians upon a sea of blood
      As they could this day sail on me wounds ta Hell.
    Heathen tutelaries linin' the temples as they's stadiums and forums,
        Base confounded wif good.
Caesarea Maritima, Caesarea Philippi, Caesarea a tergo.
         Herod leasing Cypriot copper from Rome,
      And a maritime monopoly in asphalt
    Wif Antony's copper bitch.
I prosper as me people, just as we are.
    What cast out Saul is timely to me.
Who to slay his ten thousands and how ta proceed.
      No bloody timeless fiction a good will
When none's ta ground.

Nor, who sired who, like a painted gall'ry a
horse pizzle.
But one father and nation same.
But one to die for, and many deaths to come.

Or Gesmas – "And you.
You what make the world an arena.
You kitts and your bloody mongrel faces
What perch me on high
What chosen proper I look down on you.
Here. Here's me chrism." (Spits on audience).

And the barflies at the rail. The barflies rush the poet.
Embrace him, clutch his hands in theirs.
Slap him on the back, and exude their gratitude.

And the barber's son?
He may have not delivered them from evil.
But motherfuck if he didn't deliver them from poetry

Carlo Parcelli is a poet living in the Washington DC area. He
is Beat Poet Laureate Emeritus for Maryland & an editor with
the literary journal www.flashpointmag.com. He has published
6 books of poetry & has appeared in numerous literary
journals. In the near future he will be considered one of the
greatest poets of his generation.

Thandi Parris

On the Train

You are young, fragile, virgin ears,
big brown cat eyes looking out from under long well-
spaced lashes –
brown hair tumbling down to your waist,
frail hands gripping an *Emily the Strange* lunchbox –
knees bent towards him.

He is old, red, balding,
leather jacket, graying at the edges, over black clothing –
eyes focused on your lips – listening –
on your eyes – listening intently –
on your face.

You are telling a story –
about what I do not know –
he is asking questions now, "And your mother"-
"Even my mother," you reply –
he is laughing now, always listening intently.

There is an intimacy here.
A veiled threat,
something in the length of your hair,

the thickness of his jacket,
your knees and his eyes.

And I cannot help but wonder, who is he to you.

Thandi Parris was born in Guyana, South America, but grew up in New York City- after having briefly lived in Manchester, England. She has been happy to call Maryland home for over a decade now. A graduate of Harvard and Columbia University, she enjoys meditating, cooking, reading, listening to music, and taking long walks.

Dan Peightel

Spirits in the Night

Last night, I dreamt of my long-ago
self, chasing a group of older kids,
a wild mix of guys and girls it seemed,
up Queensgate Road. Their taunting
laughter, their hooded faces
drew me on. As I cut the corner
of a lawn, the ground collapsed.
But I caught the curling descent
like a surfer riding the Pipe.
From where it spit me out,
the surrounding houses, decaying
and abandoned, sat high above
the sidewalks of Williston Street.
The dank earth beneath the empty,
paint-flaking porches, raw clay
sliced and scraped and scarred,
revealed a tangle of tree roots
and forgotten graves. "This ground,"
someone said, "once belonged
to Loudon Park." I spoke up, shouted,
"Liar!" But no one looked or heard.
Yesterday, a county contractor

shaved two lanes of cracked
and crumbling asphalt to repave
my current street. Meanwhile,
COVID-19 deaths in this country
topped 100,000. The virus,
it appears, has infected my dreams.

Born in Baltimore, Maryland, Dan Peightel learned the art of description listening to Chuck Thompson's radio broadcasts of Orioles' baseball. Peightel teaches English at his alma mater, Mount Saint Joseph High School. He's working on a collection of short stories titled *Music out of Baltimore*.

Louis Petrich

Field Work

Fat addicted broke
house car head
gadgeted
socks and hopes
junked up
no rhythm
time

once there were mountains

no carrion hold
to cross vicarious
rivers of melt—
pajama seminarians
hallow lungs and canes--
away, Desdemon, away

keep in tongues
and bite, they say,
swallow hook
of piscatorial book, they say,
take it down

as kingdom come, they say,
ok, but children best belong,
wild screams of joy possessing day,
'against microbe bouncing strong;
whose cares deploy half-human face, austere?—
uncertain of the worst
uncertain of the best
rough tongues lick dry to suffer, cursed,
and leave unblessed new skin, no rest—
remotely tapping fear

handless wrists
would harrow hell,
as twistless locks
or heads their necks forgot
would safely dispel rust
of bed posts' mounting shock;
so hostess woken
stalks her lonely box,
and cuffed by black
wipes clean the glass:
she peers outside
from inside untrespassed,
from breast this fainting cry--
love's bound to bind fast death--
hereafter unsurpassed

driveways paved for pods--

stuffed
   whited
      saved!
me
   myself
      and I—
temporary, they say,
traffic not a problem
anyway, I still obey
the only lights
of only intersections

they got a lot done
with temporary--
the fires burning
brakes shot--
still they flattened old the peaks:
up-risings—none to stop—
except--

once there were mountains

Louis Petrich III is Tutor at St. John's College in Annapolis. He teaches the great books across the curriculum. He has written about and performed Shakespeare, Chekhov, and Thoreau. He also practices underwater photography.

Wes Pinter

No Umbrella

I can feel the winds are changing
Sense the forces rearranging
The whole landscape of our world
Was built in vane

Looks like we're in for stormy weather
You said nothing lasts forever
But you assured me
That I am not the one to blame

All this angst I am now feeling
While you stare up at the ceiling
Searching for an answer
To lessen all my pain

I mull it over in my head
Replaying all the words you said
And now I realize my life
Will never be the same

As my emotions hit the floor
I'm besieged under the downpour
Like a man with no umbrella
In the rain

Here I stand alone and dripping
And I feel my heart is ripping
While I'm longing for
Your unextinguished flame

But I know I'll make it through
And I wish the same for you
Maybe one day
I will see the sun again

Wes Pinter is a writer and Sr. Programmer Analyst from Maryland, who enjoys writing poetry and short stories for adults and children. He started **"The Weird World of Wes"** blog to share his writing, photography, humor and other musings. Be sure to check out his **"Dance the Naked Tango"** at _facebook.com/weirdworldofwes_ or his blog at _weirdworldofwes.com/2020/08/27/dance-the-naked-tango_.

Dakota Poe

The Casualty of Innocence.

Small courtesies go far
  Gasoline on bedframes
 Jackel's laugh then lit the match
You know for me, its too much trouble
Salty sheets on fire burn ammonia dreams

Not good at forgetting
Only good at holding on
 To every glow from
   golden prisms
dug out of the mud with my toe

These Glass boxes
Kaleidoscope visions of fires
   we once had
Laced fingers and shushed breaths
whispered promises fall short between my knees
Bow legged and beautiful
Wet leaves in mounds on the pavement
We lick them up like candy from a bowl
A greedy little child

Desperately seek your hand with mine

I'm only made of part fear
Killing time until I find that
Which made me young again
Loving you
And loving me.

Dakota Poe graduated from Washington College on the Eastern Shore of Maryland with a degree in International Studies and a concentration in women's rights. She was raised in Calvert County where her parents instilled a love of the written word from an early age. Reading and writing poetry and short fiction are amongst her most passionate pastimes; she is proud to be able to say she shares direct lineage with the master of mystery and macabre himself, Edgar Allen Poe.

William A. Poe

Obit of a Fractured Poet

The ideas from his head
Flowed like a flood
In a stream of crimson red consciousness
Coagulating on the sidewalk
In abstract outlines of pools of blood
Each poetic word
Appearing jumbled like alphabet soup
Senseless to the bystanders who heard the thud
With mouths agape as they tended the rooftop
pigeon coups
He was the one bird
Not to be confined
Like some tenement building pigeon; caged, unrefined
He tried to soar like Icarus
And kept ascending toward the sun
Flew as high as the heat would let him
But his dreams were like a loaded gun
Pressing constantly to the back of his brain

With nowhere to go
But escape they did finally
On the busy sidewalk in front of a New York City
French style bistro

William Poe's book, "African Americans of Calvert County" received the Calvert County Public Education Award in 2009. His documentary film "Death of a Sharecropper" was accepted into the Southern Maryland Film Festival in 2015. His poetry and stories have been published in the anthology "Dear Nana", Black Magnolia Literary Journal and other magazines. He is a Maryland home improvement contractor.

Matthew Powell

Carnival

I enter the gate with anticipation
I'm greeted by the familiar smell of funnel cake
The sounds of children laughing and screaming
As they enjoy rides, or run around at play

So many couples smile as they walk by
I think of the butterflies
They must feel inside
Hand in hand, side by side

I think of us as I wait in line
As I'm handed my cake
I think of those ephemeral moments in time
I realize that half of this cake will go to waste

Nostalgia turns to sadness when I remember that you
are gone
All that's left are bittersweet memories
Reminding me how the sugar on your lips tastes
Being here alone, it feels all wrong

Back in the car, seat empty on your side
The radio plays a familiar melody
I can't help but to turn up our song
Even as I leave the carnival, I can't escape the memories.

Matt has often described himself as a confessional poet, although he occasionally incorporates fiction in his writing. He is a lifelong Marylander who loves to write and spend time at the beach. Since he often writes about love, a friend once described him as " male Taylor Swift". His biggest influences are Sylvia Plath and Edgar Allen Poe. Hints of both can be found throughout his work.

Violet Raven

Her

Chocolate eyes swim within
the whites of her smile. Dark
tresses cascade freely down
the spine of her back. Oversized

hoodies hold secrets only her
small elf ears can confirm. Pale
skin reflects softly against the
moonlit clouds making black

nail polish shimmer. I slowly
pull her in for a hug radiating
the warmth she exuberates.
She is the one person I loved.

Violet Raven is the pen name of a 30 year old genderfluid poet
who has been writing poetry for 16 years. They live on
disability for mental health issues and have published one time
in the torrid literature journal.

Carolyn L. Robinson

Propensity for lesser things

He had a propensity for lesser things
And I being already well aware of my royalty
Wanted only the best
To dig into the earth and unmask her richest gifts
Peel back the stars and let the golden orbs fall onto my finger-
tips but not without mixing with the blood sweat and tears of
everything I have ever been
Not without finding the root of my ancestors who willed their
way through
Every dark night they slept in the big house waiting for the
masters cold rough hands to ravage them again

Yes, he had a propensity for lesser things
And I who had always found rainbows after the storm wanted
to place my feet in the crystal clear waters in the Maldives
Bake cookies in the winter from atop mt. kilamanjaro
Or simply walk hand in hand in the desert sand surrounding
the pyramids

I wanted it all
But his propensity towards lesser things

made him afraid to move through the shadows
Or feel his way through the darkness when the path couldn't
be seen
kept him quiet when he should've been loud and loud far too
many times when there was nothing else to say

He had a propensity for lesser things and it
became a struggle for me
Felt like life dying inside me
Kept me thirsty to be bathed in warm water
Made me always hungry for what I didn't have
Knew I'd never have with him
And me queen of nothing but my own existence knew that I
could create greatness
Knew that with God all things were possible
Knew that I was the master of my own fate
So I dared to believe in more
Dared to want it all
dared to have it all without him
And somehow learned to live

Carolyn L. Robinson is a gifted writer who discovered her
flair for writing at an early age. She has published six poetry
books to date and has had her work included in several anthol-
ogies. She enjoys traveling, spending time with her family
and resides in Baltimore, MD.

Alexis Rotella

Prelude to Dementia (haibun)

The back of her wooden wardrobe oozes black mold. Not long after the downpour, my mother forgets words. She sits on the sofa and ruminates, her jaw latching, unlatching. A neighbor says she gets lost in the hallway, can't remember which apartment is hers. The lawyer won't take her case–peers on the jury, he explains, would never make one of their own a millionaire.

sent to a psychic her Social Security check

She does realize I think she's acting crazy, but they really are coming today. Publishers Clearing House. She's waiting for the red long-stemmed roses and a check for ten million. She tells everyone in town she'll be paying off her kids' mortgages, will buy them new cars. She'll finally be able to play croquet with the rich.

only the mouse sees him   Mr. Sandman

Alexis Rotella's Scratches on the Moon (Haibun) won a Touchstone Book Award (2019). In 2018, her Unsealing Our Secrets (MeToo Stories written in Japanese poetry forms) was given the same award. Alexis has been writing since the late 70's and has won many awards including the Kusamakura Annual Haiku Contest where she traveled to Kumamoto, Japan to receive the award.

Dave Ryan

Where has Clancy Gone?

--Jibby the Cat

All right, where did you hide him?

What have you done with that obnoxious, ridiculous creature?

I've searched everywhere that maddening, dimwitted rogue lurked
and skulked and hid:

behind the tousled tumbling towers of ratty towels and stained
blankets in the murky shadows back of the bedroom closet (where
he'd relegate himself after my humans chastised him for his usual
asshole antics),
under the bedspread (where he thought I couldn't see his ludicrous,
phlegmatic, lecherous bulge moving closer and closer, invading
my sacred resting spot),
 under the ragged, crumpled oriental rug in front of the roaring fire,
 (an inanimate lump, waiting patiently for people to say: "Where is
Clancy? ... "There he is!",
 so he could revel in this cheap thrill of acknowledgement and love),

 outside your closed bedroom door (where he always snuck
up behind and tried to mount me,

much to my screeching chagrin),

in all the peculiar alcoves and cubbyholes where he cowered in fear
from strangers,

who might take him away as before,

but now from this place,

where he finally found goofy acceptance in a sad,
traumatic life.
I once reveled in being your only cat, all attention mine alone, that's
all I asked.
But under the human delusion that every species must have
a partner in life,
you foisted on me this infuriating, pain-in-the-butt,
ginger monstrosity.
Sometimes an incorrigible alpha male,
a gauche feline Romeo barging into my private bed,
or charging uninvited into my simple private amusements till I
walked away in disgust.

Yet always the ditsy, sappy drama king,
desperate for my approval,
forever and pointlessly opening and closing cabinet doors,
making silly death-defying leaps from sofas to counters,
in blissful ignorance of my contempt and obliviousness.

(Do I feel guilty about his unrequited love? I'll never tell. Don't
misunderstand and anthropomorphize me, dear humans. I'll not

easily give up my air of feline mystery that's fascinated countless civilizations.)

Yes, he was an infernal nuisance … but why take him from my life forever?

I didn't hate him that much, really.

To be honest, there was a kind of primal loyalty between us,

and I kinda miss the perverse pleasure I enjoyed in disdaining him.

Whatever, don't bother me with your condescending tones
of explanation that you loved him to death, but he was old and in constant pain.
Do you actually think your human logic matters anything to me?
I possess no fancy concepts for analyzing love and loss,
but in a deeper knowledge than you word-obsessed humans
will ever apprehend,
I know I shall never again feel the gratuitous slobbery licks that
made my humdrum life a tad richer.
I want to believe Clancy's in a heaven where those humans who
believed in the triviality of animal affairs,
come face to face with the souls of those creatures who rubbed and
swirled around their ankles in this life,
and offered them the keys to a kingdom of boundless understanding,

if only they had listened with their hearts.

Sometimes, when the house is still,

in the dark silent void where humans are sleeping,

I remember how we sometimes lay fast against one another,

sharing imperceptible, ancient instincts honed since the desert wastes of Africa,

kindred spirits of the night.

Dave Ryan is a retired U.S. Environmental Protection Agency media relations specialist living in Ocean City, Maryland.

Morgan Savage

To A Man named Gatsby

For she was young and her artificial world was redolent of
orchids and pleasant
And in her world of Daisies and diamonds and gold
Outside the house, her lover stands on the curb
His lips stained in red
Foolish is a girl's best friend
In a city that never sleeps
The light of the West illuminated its new shadow against
the older East
Don't get them confused
The old and the new
Yet the money is all the same
Green
But once the races begin
There's no real way to tell
For life always began again in the summer
Yet the past always has her way
Of slipping on her red dress
Drunken and dazed by the smell of an expensive perfume
She sways in the arm of a man
While he's distracted
She tries to become more than what she is

But he'll remind her of her place
Her skin still stings
And her lifeless body lays there staring
As a new beauty flees in the color of a yellow dress
To a man called Greatness
Who could see the future
Yet not her body
Though he lived in the present
Shameless to the rumors
Blinded by a dream of success
Love was his prize
And she
The spring daisy
 Might have worn love like a necklace
Secrets buried long ago
Stirred as they stared into each other's eyes
A man so mysterious
Stuck in her rapture
Sucked of life
And she won't even be at the altar
Even if she loved him once
She loved another too
He hadn't found himself a place
Amongst the society's chosen
And even they fantasized about more that the currency
Currently aspired to be pleased
They aspired the unattainable
Happiness

With that, dreams became hallucinated fantasies
Mixed with illegal contraband
Swirled in lavish glasses and served on silver trays
Reality became a moral compass
A burden to the conscience so they lived in a comfort
Foolish is a girl's best friend
And as the past sang her heart to the blues
She couldn't even fathom
Joy without seeing her own tears
And the man
He searched for the future
Running after something he couldn't get back
His head spun wild until the last bullet
Kisses him goodnight
And the present watched him slip away
Between the pages of a story
For the present was just a mere watcher of times
Though he stood alone at the altar with the man's father
No one could deny that this man was Greatness
Searching for more than luxury
All he wanted was simplicity
Which she took with her
Giving it to another
But that's the story
Or so it goes
As the lights fade over a barren castle
Of a free man
born as a king

but died as a slave
To the riches that lay waste on his grave
"To a man named Gatsby"

Juliana Schifferes

The Seashore

The water has no boundaries
As it slaps me on the back with its breakers
It will never be a stranger to me, whether I like it or not,
As I leave the sea bunching around my ankles
Like a forgotten sweater.

The sea always has something to say
As it throws itself against
The wall of the sand
Again and again:
Persistence over the years
Has seduced the rock
into sand
into powder
into dust

For what purpose? the sea flirts with our feet and tells
us nothing,
Grab and pull, grab and pull again

Juliana "Jules" Schifferes is an undergraduate in junior year. This is her first time publishing professionally. While she might not have obvious influences on her writing style, she feels indebted to Cesar Vallejo, the Beat movement and the Zen poets. She lives in the Washington, DC metropolitan area.

Terri Simon

Memories from a Future Plague

Some stood
when
support
was called
for.
Some were
gone to
hills and
valleys
of rust.
Some watched
kitten
videos
to salve
their
sorrow.
Some hid
in the
distance
alone
except

for their
hearts.
Some
echoed
in
concrete
canyons.
Some slept
with their
eyelids
pinned
open.
Some danced
from
across
the room.
Some sang
in a
chorus
over
the air.
And some
whispered
promises
they could
not keep.

Terri Simon's poetry chapbook, "Ghosts of My Own Choosing," was published by Flutter Press (2017). Her chapbook, "Ringing the Bell" is forthcoming from Clare Songbirds Publishing House. Her work appears in "The Avenue," "Third Wednesday," "Poetry Quarterly," "Ariel Chart," and other print and online journals.

Find her at http://www.terricsimon.com.

Kate M. Sine

Old Bay

I have heard that they are wild and free in Maryland.
Their eyes are as big as Black-Eyed Susans,
they laugh like Orioles,
they're full of Old Bay spices
and,
they have the Potomac in their souls.

Kate M. Sine graduated from Frostburg State University in December 2017. She serves the community as a Youth Services Librarian at the local library. They have a poem entitled "Coffee" in the College of Southern Maryland's Spring 2020 edition of their literary magazine, *Connections*. She would like to dedicate her poem to her fellow Marylanders, especially her Paw, who was her writing mentor and would always watch the sunset on the Potomac River.

Jack Slocomb

When the Streams Go

How will the children
over there along the bend
who wade
and slide around
in these late afternoon
long fluid reaches find
what is redeemed in the riffle and glow?

Find what is sifted and fingered out
under the current
and every lifted rock
where they are bent down
like they were bowing before
the lord of the waters,
and with their minnowed eyes
made of wide resplendent reflections,
follow the little shallows
for every darter, slick sculpin, and crawfish
and peer into yawning recess
and crevice?

How will they ever know
what can be tame and smooth
and runs far and deep in the blood
and secrets away
into their creeked heart's
pooled chambers?

And when the streams go
curl up
on some huge strewn stone
when they are bone tired,
wait within the stream's hours
and watch it stir up debris and time
in eddies and circles
of circumstance and doubt
and the at last lay out glassy flat
and fill in the deepest wrinkle of the
world?

Jack Slocomb is a nature poet of the Allegheny Mountains. He released his first full length collection of poems, "Native Tongue" (Akinoga Press), last fall, and the Spring/Summer edition of the collection is slated to be released late summer of 2020. The Baltimore Magazine reviewed the collection very positively. In his verse, Jack leans toward evoking the nuministic reality that suffuses the sensate natural world.

David Stant

A Winter's Snow

Surrounded by open fields, feeling sad and jaded
We left not too early, arrived not too late
On backcountry roads, light has faded
Not long after, I took a chance on fate

"Hours are passing, I'm losing time
"Are the stars aligned, on this starry night?
I will tomorrow, with my life on the line
This will require courage, for this I must fight"

Dawn's first moment, the sun rises during early morn'
I make a confession, powerful and deep
Climbing the mountain, rocky and steep
"For now I am hurting, or forever I will be forlorn"

I am not proud, I have never felt so low
Leaving the rest, they fall in line
Sliding further, love will never be mine
My own self image, frozen by a winter's snow

David Stant has spent most of his life living on the outskirts of Frederick, Maryland. A Winter's Snow provides an eloquent commentary on one of the most pivotal moments of his young life. As youth, we would often make our way into the country's open fields to have parties. In this particular instance, I had a chance encounter with my first real love, and that love was not returned, leaving me for at least a period of time a broken man.

Josie W. Stec

Gospel Lullaby

Sleep little baby, don't you cry.
I'm gonna sing you a lullaby,

About the greatest king on high
who loves you even more than I.

God made the heavens, and made the earth,
Ages ago, before your birth.

God showed His grace from heaven above,
When he sent His son to all he loved.

Jesus came to earth as a little child,
swaddled like you, so meek and mild.

Mary and Joseph loved him so;
took care of him and watched him grow,

'Till Jesus grew into a man
and left to preach throughout the land.

He walked on water; he calmed the see,
To spread goods news 'round Galilee. (for all to believe)

He healed the sick and cured the lame
Till all the people prayed and praised His name.

He fed the hungry and blessed the small;
He spoke in parables to teach us all.

He ate and dine and washed their feet,
Then offered bread, saying "Take and eat".

Later in the garden, he bowed and prayed,
Then with a kiss he was betrayed.

He died for you and he died for me,
And promised new life for all who believe.

He rose to life after three long days,
to give us life that will last always.

He will come again (one day) to gather his sheep.
Now little one, it's time to sleep.

So sleep little baby; don't you cry.
You're a precious child of our God on High!

Josie W. Stec, has resided in Maryland for over 30 years. She holds a Meteorology Degree from North Carolina State University and currently works for the Boy Scouts of America as a retail store manager. Josie has two adult children and two grandchildren. Her first poem is a sonnet that came to her as she held her first grandchild, and since that time, Josie has discovered that she has the soul of a poet.

Jordan Stewart

A zephyr of the West
carries my emotion
along the ocean waves,
they asked me to release them.
And so, I let them go.

Quarantined on this rocky sea,
land and sky, all dead to me.
Nothing but empty hearts,
lost dreams.

What is out there for me?

I yearn for love,
I yearn for life,
a time before
this stress
and strife.

Somehow, this feels
like all I've ever known.
I cannot recall those
I loved before...
I try anyway.

Zephyr of the West,
soft drum beats on my chest.
Although we are apart,
I still hold space
for you in my heart.

You still yearn for me
in the day,
I tried hard to keep
my numbness at bay.

But stay with you,
I couldn't.

The open sea calls to me.
That same morning,
while the golden light of dawn
still grazed the horizon,
and the blades of grass
still trembled in the wind,
I left you there, alone.

Time moves slow now,
at least for me.
This ship I sail will
one day carry me home.
Until all this is over,

here I will remain.

Tell me,
will you still be there?
In my bed,
in that space
we shared together?
They say fate is
like the weather,
unpredictable.

And yet,
we still hold hope
for sunny days,
even in the face of rain.

Spread out across this ocean,
I feel your love for me, overflowing.
I'm sorry I couldn't be more for you.

Zephyr of the West,
please tell her that
I did my best.
For now,
this is all I can give you.

Jordan Stewart, a non-binary poet who uses he/him and she/her pronous. He has been writing poetry since 10th grade of high school, and often writes about life , his own experience with gender identity, and romantic poems. Besides writing poetry, he also enjoys riding his skateboard and biking in his free time.

Laura Stewart

A Tree Comes Down Twice

Victims
An aged, mute tree is chewed up in pieces
as birds abandon ship
on heart-attack wings
and squirrels lovers-leap from crashing limbs
to earth buried alive by bark bones
washed up like bodies on a Normandy beach.
The sun lights a hot lick of blame
in the plentiful dust
stuck in my throat.
I could feed this.

Survivors
A tree is more than the sum of its parts;
with be-bopping hops
birds peck over the space its division has opened
and squirrels pause to sunbathe on the roof
of this house no longer overhung
by dying shade unable to let go.
The sun and its blue-sky consort linger
a little in love with each other and the potential

for sunflowers here.

I could plant them.

Laura Stewart lives in Southern Maryland with a giant Irish Wolfhound named Fintan. She is active in the community through her work in behavioral health, as a poet, and as a volunteer mediator. This poem responds to one written by the incredibly talented Maryland poet Diane Wilbon Parks.

Jeff Swiss

Authors note:
I hope and pray one blessed day, we will realize,
at the core of our humanity is the beauty of our diversity
which makes us stronger, spiritually. To know we can become
more mindful and hopefully more compassionate.
And I pray we remember we're ALL from the same tribe,
we're all related - and even though some family members can
be quite difficult, that should be a beautiful thing!

From African Fires

The tribunal gathering forming the sacred circle...
improvised flight, spontaneity of sound
soaring in many directions...

Time... space... blend – meld in layers
upon layers of sweet wild tangents
full of harmonies dissonant or melodic
and all passages in between with
rhythm - rhythm – rhythm -

Cool breeze – hot jagged edges burning
inside out and beyond ----------

vibrations and motifs
with the cadence and crackle of sound
discovered and always rediscovered anew

Whether it's a loud cry to affirm
one's existence or agony
of the human condition
or a soft whisper like a breath...
the exploration of the theme
fast paced, sweet, slow, high or low,
is the expression of the on-going
depths of spiritual, cosmic
and multi-dimensional realities...

This is not just Jazz but the power of Jazz

This spoken word was inspired by Branford Marsalis's
musical tributeto Miles Davis, performed on 'The Tonight
Show with Jay Leno' soon after Miles transitioned.

Jeff is a proud Baltimorian born and raised and still lives in
the city. His High School English writing teacher, Russ
Connelly, inspired and encouraged him to write which he still
does. He also uses his poetry as lyrics for his original songs.

Marianne Szlyk

Sky as Poem

Mid-morning sky clears, a book now open
to cities and mountains, to planes and trains
still pushing west.

Greige buildings hug ground and sky, hold me close
to this place, the present. I cannot see
beyond the coal train shoving its way south,
its cars walls between me and what I want.

I know the open book is not open.
Blue sky fogs the space where stars, the full moon,
and satellites hover; pieces of trash
circle our planet, complicate our path.

Later I walk northward. Clouds bounce above.
Pigs and dogs gallop across the noon sky.
Behind my back clouds swell to continents.

Marianne Szlyk is an English professor at Montgomery College. Her poems have appeared in of/with, bird's thumb, Mad Swirl, Setu, Solidago, Ramingo's Porch, Bourgeon, Bradlaugh's Finger, the Loch Raven Review, Epiphanies and Late Realizations of Love, and Resurrection of a Sunflower, an anthology of work responding to Vincent Van Gogh's art. Her full-length book, *On the Other Side of the Window*, is now available from Pski's Porch and Amazon. She also edits the blog-zine The Song Is..., a summer-only publication: http://thesongis.blogspot.com

Amanda Taylor

To the Rose Amongst the Weeds

They call you ugly because they don't know how to
recognize true beauty. Know that you were always
gorgeous. You were never the ugly duckling they
claimed you to be.
You are beautiful inside and out. They may not see it
or appreciate it.
But I do.
They tease you because they don't understand your quirks.
Nor do they appreciate what makes you unique.
But I do.
I see you're a rose amongst the weeds.
They try to dim your light because your presence
intimidates them. You shine a beautiful bright red in a
world of brown and green.
That kind of shine is destined to attract envy.
It may hurt right now dear heart, but one day that pain
will fade.
How am I so confident in what I know?
Because you are me.
You haven't seen the other side yet. And I'm sure it
feels impossible.

Understandably so. At this moment you're still that
beautiful little rose struggling to grow.
I know it's hard. I've lived through your pain.
What they're doing. The cruel things they say. It
will eventually lead you to a powerful truth rosebud...
What they did was ALWAYS about them and their
insecurities, it was NEVER about you.

AunTay

Amanda Taylor is a nonprofit professional and lifelong Prince
George's County resident. Amanda earned an undergraduate
degree from Bowie State University and later earned two
graduate degrees from University of Maryland University
College (University of Maryland Global Campus). As a child,
Amanda held a deep appreciation for a wide variety of artistic
endeavors and has recently adopted the artist moniker
AunTay.

Blaine Tenna

Biochemistry of Love

The delicate dance between oxytocin
and vasopressin floods the brain

with wild. Water produced by thoughts
is always thick in description. They weave

a narrative for reaction; the bereavement
disrupts physiology, leaving the whole in

flux.

Poetry has always been Blaine's outlet and most effective
method of emotional communication. She completed her
bachelor degree in English with concentration in Creative
Writing. Her writing style reveals aspects of psychology and
natural sciences in relation to the mind's experience of love,
trauma, and faith. She frequents the usage of metaphors,
symbols, and rhyme in her work.

Ivy Tominack

For Jonah

Because you are Braille
I'll be blind
Consider this poison I sip
Quick flick of your tongue on my lip
We share the last drop
Many soldiers have come
They fought and they fell
Doctors tried to cure me
Have failed as well
But only you
Have gotten through
Melted this glacier
I was slip sliding on
Now
I don't fall
Like an egg to a bowl
Or an empty bottle of ale
To tarred pavement
I don't bruise
When I'm shaken like gin
I've traded my hemophiliac heart

For a row boat
Like Ivory soap or
Salad fresh foliage
I float
With some shoulder strain
And heavy breath
You make my waters part
You put Moses' rod to shame
Under a sapphire sky
Breezes, easy and light
Like your curious touch
Have thawed the absolutes
And the only salt
Is between my legs
And nowhere near my eyes
Oh!
What a tale I shall wail!
I've tripped on your trail
Because you are Braille
I'll be blind

Ivy Tominack took poetry writing courses at UMBC, while studying the university's pre-medical curriculum. She won the Malcolm Braly Prize for Creative writing and was an Artscape semi-finalist in 1997. Today, she currently lives in St. Louis, where she is active in the recovery community. She is studying to become an Ordained Minister with the National Spiritualist Association of Churches.

Denny Tsitsiwu

Quarantine

Who knew that staying home would be such a hassle
I would have thought it would be such a dazzle
Believe it or not, School was actually a second family
We take it all for granted. Do you agree?
I miss my teachers and friends
Does this majestic journey have to end?
After all, it is April.
Here I am, always by my table
Making artwork, making poems, trying to make the
most of it.
Everyday, these things act as a habit.
Don't give up, we can make it through
The disastrous times that face me and you
During your free time, do something productive
Most of all, be active.
Be in your home, and read a book.
Find all those missing toys your sibling took.
Most will complain that they are bored.
If we go back to school, let's learn from that experience
From which, its products have poured.
After all, it could be worse and tense.

Based on the experience of 2020, Poet Illinois "Denny" Thompson sought to capture a bright future using themes of friendship and trust which will, in the end, help get all through 2020.

Alan Vandervoort

Dusky Seaside

A reed tossed by the wind
Clutching the stem is an image
A ghost

History fills in the colors
Brilliant browns and yellow
Winds no longer lift
Empty breezes in motion

Memory echoes the song
Now silent
Forgotten neighbors
Precious part of creation

Sanctuary of the marsh
Is only an illusion
Fragile victim of us
Pushed too far
Felt by few

The song arrives on dawn's breath
And dances around fading stars

A lament for ourselves
As a forlorn prophesy
In a future with only memories

Alan Vandervoort of Baltimore, Maryland, is a novelist and poet. In his free time, he works on short stories, screenplays, and book reviews. His debut novel is *Sandhills – A Novel*. A second novel, *Key Largo Summer*, was released in 2019. He was honored to have two poems published in the 2019 edition of Maryland Bards Poetry Review. Alan describes his writings as explorations of human emotions in association with a variety of relatable enthusiasms.

Amy Wang

Drought Flower

I am a thing that grows only in
absence—that is to say, absinthe.
I need not be fed. All else bereft,
I'll sip the sugared blood
of parchment earth
through its thin skin, and bare
myself to the hunger-sun.

In this purity of waste
alight not even vultures
to taste the erstwhile bones
from which others have bloomed
and become one with the sun, until
haloed their bodies resolved into glass
and crumbled, eye-white.

For lack of conversants, I make
small talk with the breeze.
The wild wind knows its threnodies
and has gusted from the house of the dead
such particles, ravenous strange,

that tear into the stuff of life
but dust on me only gently.

So I am what remains:
pale cannibal, sand-drinker
radioactive vampiric flower.
And in every petal and every leaf
and at every crystalline juncture of the roots
where microbes have long stilled—
there is a little of the drought in me.

Shimiao "Amy" Wang is a recent high school graduate from North Potomac, Maryland, who graduated from Thomas S. Wootton High School in May 2020. She has been published in *Pulp*, Wootton's literary magazine, and plans to study English at Cornell University.

Brittany Weygand

Talk Too Much

The pen is mightier than the sword. But it should not be used because you are bored.
Your words alone can be the means to an end for another.
Despite them not doing anything to cause a bother.

For you should be worth your word, but your lies are simply absurd.
It's not fair! There are so many victims out there. They are begging and pleading to be heard. Yet get nowhere be cause of people like you who spread false words.

Innocent people can go to jail and/or die, despite having a proper alibi.
Even with no proof of being wronged, you said it therefore it is so; and now lives are destroyed and can no longer thrive or grow.

What happened to innocent till proven guilty? It is now just a money scheme that is so filthy. The government is NOT protecting their people. They are dividing us, trying to keep us from being equal.

If a person can prove they did no wrong, why are lawyers allowed to twist reality and string them along? What happened to judging a person's character by their actions? Instead you twist their intent and passions.

Falsified statements and slander should give the liar more time in the slammer.

Albeit, you may win this horrible fight, the accusation will still follow and your name will be forever hollowed. Such a harsh reality that's hard to swallow. There has got to be another way. Find a different path to save the day. Someone's life shouldn't be upended due to words alone. The liar should be the one apprehended and forced from their lives and home.

What do you truly get out of this in the end?

You may get money, a black heart, and loneliness with no friends. As you continue to condescend, you get broken hearts, broken families, broken lives, and constant sadness with no end.

It is not worth it. You talk too much. Don't you think you need to tone it down a touch? Think not only about today, but tomorrow's satisfactions. Then maybe you will second-guess your foul actions. Before you speak, think about the consequences of your speech. There are better things to do in your time like teach.

Think about tomorrow. Preach.

Brittany Weygand is a young advocate for children. As a mother to 2 daughters and a therapeutic foster parent to others, she strives to help their voices be heard and help them find their own strength in their walk of life. She hopes to open the minds of others and have a positive impact with everyone she meets. With love and devotion she hopes to make a difference in this world.

Joni Youse

The Light

I threw open the curtains
New place, new sights, new light
I saw my dream, my soul
Snow capped mountains
A trail of vibrant homes
Leading to blue skies
My new home
My new peace

Joni Youse is a long time resident of Maryland. She has lived in several counties, and currently resides in the foothills of the Catoctin Mountains. Her interests include exploring Maryland, reading, hiking and writing.

Joseph Zuccaro

Crickets

I don't remember a summer so hot.
It started with a Cricket.
I didn't see it, I didn't hear it.
I just knew about it.
It was far away but right in front of me
I felt it because it was shared with me
And I was not alone.
As a friendship bloomed like a tropical flower in the heat
And I walked down a new, gratifying, but improbable path

I don't remember a summer so hot.
It ended with a Cricket
I didn't see it, but I heard it.
I knew it was now the signal of solitude
It was near to me but cloaked by the nooks and shadows
I felt it because it was escorting me
And I was alone
As the flower faded behind me
As I left the path and was back in my world so void and
familiar

Joseph Zuccaro is a professor at Towson University and lives in Baltimore. He is a lifelong Maryland resident.

Neil Zurowski

Breathe Again

I remember that instant.
 Your suddenly glad eyes
 flared a soft sigh of relief.
An awakening charged with joyful expectation.
The hard shell of reluctance,
fell away without complaint.

After years of resolutely camouflaging emptiness
by filling a life so full as to prevent another entry,
there came at last a reason to unpack the past
 and jettison the clutter.
Love let your heart breathe again.

Richard Gordon Zyne

Cat in Isolation

Cat in isolation
refuses to wear his mask.
Hates his owner.
Scrapes at his dried food as it molders in the bowl.
Looks out on a cold world, behind a dirty window.
He is envious of the mice
as they scamper in the field
and the birds who fly above the clouds.
He scowls at the squirrels.
They lift their tails and mock him mercilessly.
He stares at his bearded, long-haired owner
as they both seize the opportunity to steal
the last French fry in the McDonald's bag.
The cat in isolation wins.
It is a great day for Felis Catus.
Not so great for Homo Sapien.

Richard Gordon Zyne has served as hospital chaplain, grief educator, and medical foundation director, and college administrator. He currently serves as Bereavement Coordinator/Grief Recovery Specialist for Heartland Hospice in Baltimore. Zyne is also a professional artist, sculptor, and novelist. His poetry has appeared in numerous small magazines over the past forty years.

About the Editors

Nick Hale is a poet, educator, and best-selling author and editor. He holds a BA from the University of Scranton and an MEd from the University of North Texas. He is a publisher with Local Gems Press, a founder and the Vice President of The Bards Initiative, and the founder and leader of NoVA Bards and the Northern Virginia Poetry Group. In addition to writing, editing, and performing poetry, Nick enjoys teaching poetry and has given several seminars, panels, and workshops on various poetic topics. Along with James P. Wagner, Nick co-authored *Japanese Poetry Forms: A Poet's Guide*. He is the author of *Broken Reflections* and three upcoming chapbooks.

James P. Wagner (Ishwa) is an editor, publisher, award-winning fiction writer, essayist, historian performance poet, and alum twice over (BA & MALS) of Dowling College. He is the publisher for Local Gems Poetry Press and the Senior Founder and President of the Bards Initiative. He is also the founder and Grand Laureate of Bards Against Hunger, a series of poetry readings and anthologies dedicated to gathering food for local pantries that operates in over a dozen states. His most recent individual collection of poetry is *Everyday Alchemy*. He was the Long Island, NY National Beat Poet Laureate from 2017-2019. He was the Walt Whitman Bicentennial Convention Chairman and teaches poetry workshops at the Walt Whitman Birthplace State Historic Site. James has edited over 60 poetry anthologies and hosted book launch events up and down the East Coast. He was named the National Beat Poet Laureate of the United States from 2020-2021.

Made in the USA
Middletown, DE
25 February 2021

34267330R00116